THE
FIRST
BOOK
OF
BUGS

Bugs Bugs

Everywhere

A special thank you to Dr. N. J. Berrill, Ph. D. Sc., F,R,S,C, Strathcona Professor of Zoology at McGill University in Montreal, not only because he carefully checked this book for its scientific accuracy, but also because he first introduced the author-artist to he adventure in a bug's world.

Thank you also to Mr. George Moore, custodian of the Lyman Entomological Collection at McGill University, and to Mrs. E. E. Terrill, Librarian of the Blackader Library of Zoology at McGill University, for their assistance.

M. W.

This edition published 2022
by Living Book Press

ISBN: 978-1-922950-73-4 (hardcover)
        978-1-922950-66-6 (softcover)

A catalogue record for this book is available from the National Library of Australia

THE
FIRST
BOOK
OF

BUGS

WRITTEN & ILLUSTRATED BY

MARGARET WILLIAMSON

about BUGS

Not all the tiny creatures you see creeping and crawling and flying are truly bugs. When somebody says, "Ooh, look at the bug!" he might be pointing at a beetle with six legs, or a spider with eight legs, or a centipede with many legs. Or he might be pointing at a stink bug, which belongs to the only family scientists call bugs. But in this book, let's call them all bugs to make it easier, and, often where a bug is magnified, the outline beside it shows you about how big it really is.

If you watch a bug as it goes along about its business, you can find out what a bug's world is like. You can see what kind of legs and wings and feelers it has and how they work, and you can hear the noises it makes.

If you wait and watch long enough, you may even see it creep out of the hard, stiff suit of armor that all bugs wear, and walk off in the new and bigger suit that has been growing, all wrinkled, underneath the old one.

If you wait still longer, you might see how a bug's young are born and how they grow up. Perhaps you may even find out who its enemies are.

mud dauber wasp

centipede

squash bug

rove beetle

Bugs are so small that it is hard to imagine they can be strong enough to fight their enemies. But some of them can run or jump quickly, while others can fly away.

mexican squash bug

A bug may have a sting, to sting its enemies, or strong jaws to bite them. Some bugs can run or jump quickly, while others can fly away. Even so, lots of bugs are killed. But there are always more. There are more bugs in the world than all the people and animals you can think of. That's mostly because bugs are born by the thousands—much faster than their enemies can eat them up.

Bugs do not think about things or make plans as people do. They are born knowing everything they need to know about getting food, and fighting their enemies, and building their houses.

stink bug

Even a young spider builds its first web perfectly, although it may never have seen another spider web. Its mother does not ever need to show it how.

Not even scientists have figured out exactly how a bug knows these things. That is still a bug's secret.

may fly

ladybugs

silverfish

Sometimes people get angry at bugs. Clothes moths chew up their swimming suits and mittens, cockroaches crawl over dishes in the sink, potato bugs eat holes in potato vines, Japanese beetles ruin the prettiest roses and termites chew wooden stairs in houses.

But bugs are valuable, too. After all, the honey for your waffles comes from bees, and silk for your dresses from silkworms, and the shellac that makes your furniture shine comes from scale bugs.

Even those same termites who tunnel through wooden stairs in our houses, eat old dead wood in other places where it is not wanted and make it part of the earth again. In that way, they save people the trouble of burning or burying lots of rubbish, and they make room for new animals and plants as well.

clothes moth

No bug really intends to be harmful or useful. It just lives its own life. Now you're going to see how some bugs live, what they eat, where they sleep, how long they live, and how they have fun.

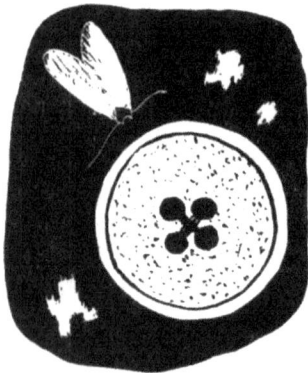

termites tunneling through wood

CRICKETS and their COUSINS

Best of all, a cricket likes to sit in the sun and make music. If he's frightened, he'll stop playing, and jump like a jumping jack.

A cricket has a fiddle and a bow hidden in his two top wings. The top of each wing has ridges on it and the bottom of each wing has a row of small teeth like a file. To make his music, he crosses his wings one over the other and saws them back and forth.

A cricket can fool you. When he plays loudly, he sounds as if he were right beside you. But he can play very softly to make himself sound far away.

In the springtime, Mr. Cricket plays a love song to a lady cricket, who listens carefully with her knees. That's where crickets' ears are. She can't play music because she has no fiddle in her wings. Besides, after a while she is busy laying dozens of eggs in holes which she digs in the earth with her sharp pointed shovel. Later, she dies, but the young crickets can get along perfectly well from the minute they are born, even while they are in the egg.

a crickets ears are in it's knees

a cricket "singing"

the file on a cricket's wing

The sun bakes the earth that covers the eggs and keeps them warm. When the young crickets have grown too big for the eggs, they push with their heads till the lids on their eggs fly open, and out they pop. They look just like grown-up crickets, but they are much smaller, and have no wings. They are curious, and push their way out of the earth to go adventuring. If they are lucky, and are not gobbled up by an ant or a lizard, crickets wander all summer long, hiding under leaves and stones, and usually waiting until night to hunt for food.

A cricket eats so much that soon its hard black suit, which cannot grow at all, splits open down the back and it creeps out in its new and bigger suit. Before the summer is over and a cricket is full-sized, it grows out of four or five suits.

In the fall, it digs itself a house in the earth. It digs and scrapes and sweeps and rakes with its legs, and lifts pebbles out of the

10

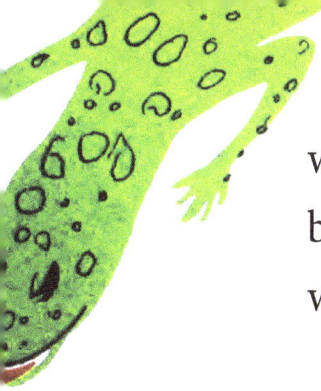

way with its strong jaws. It hollows out a tunnel just big enough to crawl through and a room at the end where it can just turn around.

A cricket's house is not where young grow up, like the bee's hive, and it is not a trap for bugs like the spider's web. A cricket's house is just for itself--a place where it can be safe and warm and snug, and it will fight fiercely if other bugs walk in by mistake.

To find a field cricket's house, try the edge of a field where the grass is not so tall. Look closely, because the front door is just a tuft of grass. If the cricket is not outside, you can bring it out by poking a straw down the tunnel.

Some crickets do not dig houses. Instead, when it gets cold they hop into people's homes and live in a crack where it is warm. In China, a friendly house cricket is often kept in a cage as a musical pet. Boys and girls carry the cages on strings around their necks and feed the crickets melon and lettuce from tiny dishes, or a spoonful of mosquitoes as medicine if their feelers droop.

Crickets have relatives who play music, too, on hot summer days and nights. The katydid plays a song which sounds like

11

a female cockroach carrying her egg case

"Katy did, Katy didn't," by rubbing his wings together, much as crickets do.

A grasshopper makes his music by rubbing the files on his back legs across the ridges on his top wings, and he listens with the ears in his sides. When grasshoppers fly, they make a crackling noise by rattling all four wings.

Some of the crickets' relatives aren't so much fun to have around. Cockroaches come into houses, crawl over food, and nibble everything in sight. The female cockroach carries around a bag with sixteen eggs inside. When she finds a warm crack to put them in, she leaves them there to hatch.

Grasshopper locusts travel in swarms as big as storm clouds in the sky. Wherever they land they eat every green, growing thing in sight. That's why farmers are so afraid of them.

The cicada, who is sometimes called a locust too, is another bug musician, but he doesn't belong to the cricket or grasshopper family. He makes his whirring noise by squeezing the muscles in and out on two drums on his stomach, just as you can make a

a katydid

noise by pushing in and out on the bulging
bottom of a pan.

As a young cicada, in a white suit, it may live
for as long as seventeen years, tunneling through
the earth, eating roots. Then it comes up to the air,
climbs a tree, splits its skin, and walks out, a grown-up cicada
with wings. No other six-legged creature takes so long to grow
up.

Some bugs eat their old skins, but the cicada leaves its skin
behind on the bark of a tree where you can find it quite easily,
if you look.

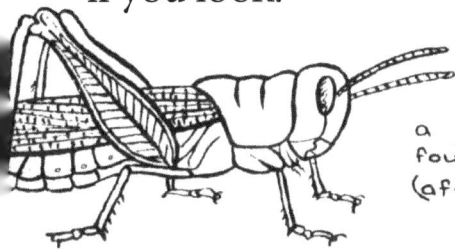

a grasshopper may change its skin
four or five times before it is grown up
(after Buchsbaum)

about BEETLES

Everywhere you go there are beetles--flying through the air, walking in the grass, or swimming in the water. They all have mouths with many parts to help them bite and chew their food and build their houses and fight their enemies. They all have coats of armor for protection, and their young all grow up in the same way.

Here is a ladybug beetle. Its orange coat of armor, like all beetle armor, is made of two wings which fit tightly over its back. These wings are very hard and they protect the two soft brown flying wings underneath. When a ladybug flies, it raises its hard wing-covers high, so that they won't be in the way.

Here is a female tiger beetle. She lays an egg in a pit she digs in the earth. When the egg hatches, out creeps a doodlebug, which looks like a worm with hooks on its back. These help it climb up and down like an elevator inside its pit. A doodlebug's head is as round and as flat as a plate and fits up into the top of its tunnel like a trapdoor. From the outside, it looks like part of the ground.

more tiger beetles

If a tiny creature does not watch where it is going, it might walk right over the doodlebug's face--and get caught in the strong jaws. Then the doodlebug takes it to the bottom of the tunnel to eat it.

For two years the doodlebug lives in its burrow, eating in the summer and sleeping in the winter, and changing its skins as

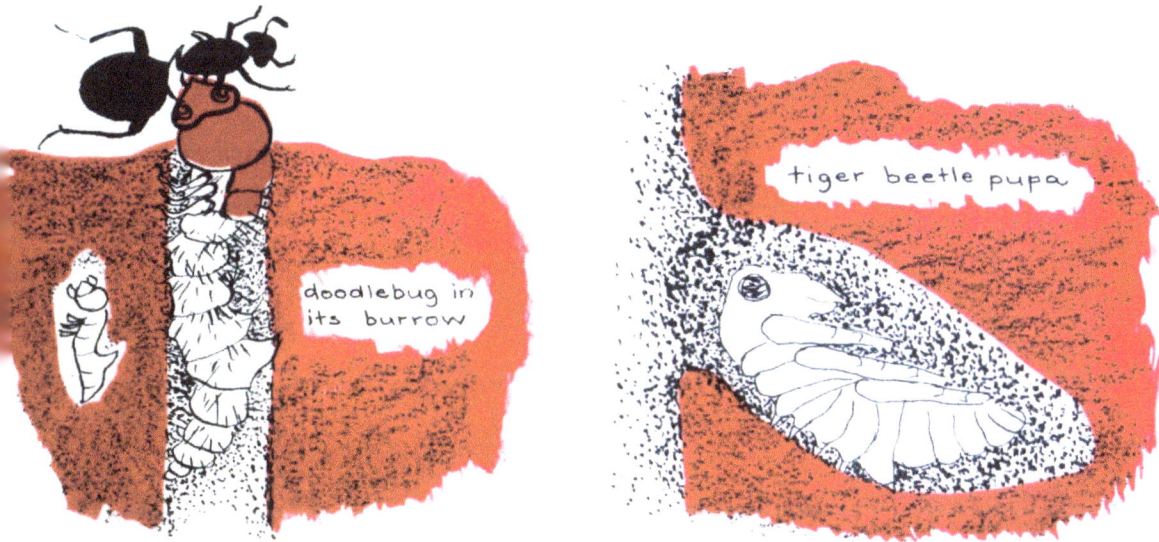

doodlebug in its burrow

tiger beetle pupa

it grows bigger and bigger. Then one day, it closes its door with earth and goes to the bottom of its tunnel and digs a bedroom off to the side. There it changes into quite a different skin from all the others it has worn. This one is called a pupa skin. As a pupa, it sleeps, all the time growing less and less like a doodlebug, and more and more like a grown-up beetle. Then one day the pupa skin splits open and a tiger beetle crawls out.

All beetles grow up like tiger beetles. A beetle is born as an egg. But it doesn't hatch first into a little beetle. Instead, a worm-like creature, usually called a larva, hatches from the egg and lives to eat and grow bigger and change its skin. When a larva changes its skin for the last time, it becomes a pupa and goes to sleep. When the pupa skin splits open, a grown-up beetle with wings and feelers and legs creeps out. How all this happens, no one exactly knows. That is another bug secret.

Though all beetles grow up in the same way and have a protecting armor and a mouth for biting and chewing, each kind of beetle has something that makes it different from all the others.

A firefly is a beetle with a light on its tail. The firefly makes two chemicals inside itself which, when they are squirted out together, glow brightly without heat. At mating time, the female's light shines extra brightly. Since only the male can fly, she climbs to the top of a bush. There she twists about all night long and flashes her light to attract the male fireflies who flit about her.

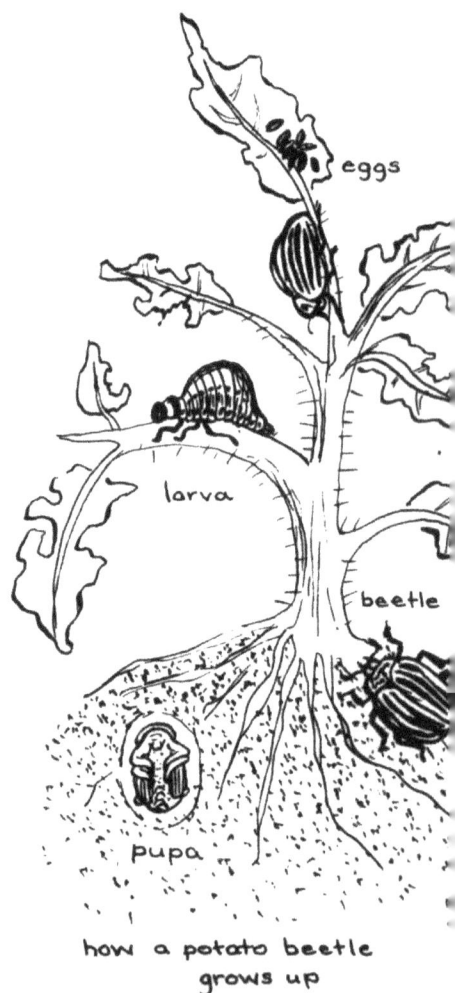

eggs

larva

beetle

pupa

how a potato beetle
grows up

Here are diving beetles. They can swim, and have things which are special to swimming beetles. Their long legs are like hairy paddles, and their bodies are streamlined to help them slip through the water. Diving beetles can't breathe under water, where they collect their food, so they store bubbles of air underneath their hard wing covers. They breathe this air through small holes along the edge of their backs.

A tumblebug beetle, also called a dung beetle, is a sculptor who makes balls of manure, which is its food. Its flat, sharp-edged head is its shovel for digging and cutting. Its front legs have teeth to use as a rake and broom, and its four back legs are curved, to shape and pat the manure into a ball. When the ball is round and just right, the tumble-bug rolls it along to a place where it can eat quietly all by itself. The bug burrows into the ground, builds a dining room, rolls its food ball in-side, and closes the

diving beetles

door with earth. When this ball is eaten, the bug starts all over again.

Sometimes a tumblebug has an accident; the ball rolls away and the bug tumbles on its back. Other times a lazy tumblebug tries to steal another bug's ball and there is a fight. If the lazy robber doesn't want to fight, it may pretend to help, by pulling the ball, or it may climb up on top and get a free ride. Then it waits for a chance to steal the ball.

In the autumn, the mother tumblebug digs a burrow and builds a very special pear-shaped ball. One end is a cradle for an egg. The other end is the food for the larva that will hatch from her egg.

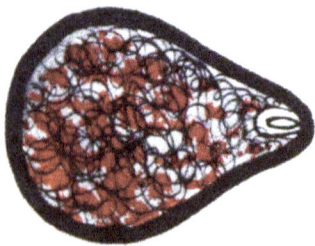

pear-shaped ball with egg

While the larva grows bigger and bigger, the food in the storehouse grows smaller and smaller, till at last the larva fills the whole pear-shaped shell. Inside this shell it turns first into a pupa, then into a full-grown tumblebug, and then it pushes its way out into the world.

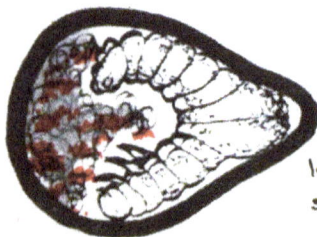

larva eating into its storehouse of food

18

cucumber beetle

rhinoceros beetle

grape weevil

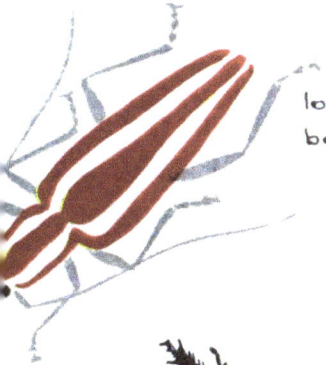

long-horned
beetle

stag beetle

tumblebug

There are many more beetles, and each one has something which is quite special to itself.

whirligig beetle

burying
beetle

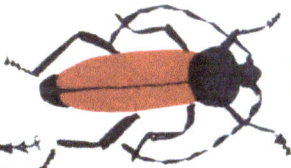

long-horned
beetle

ground beetle

click beetle

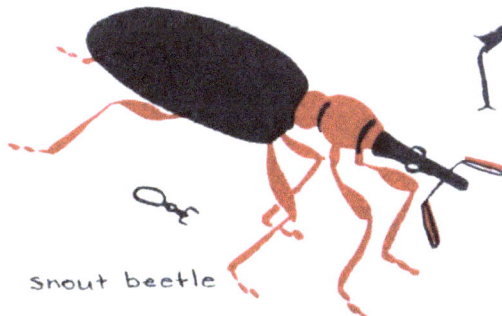

snout beetle

about *FLIES*

The fly we know best is the housefly. There are many other kinds, too. Flies are called flies because they can fly farther and better and faster than almost all other bugs with wings. A true fly has two wings, and it zooms in a straight line. Each wing has a stiff strong front edge, but the main part of the wing is thinner than cellophane. As its wings move up and down, the air pushes against the thin part and makes it bulge like a sail in the wind. The bigger the bulge, and the oftener the fly's wings move up and down, the faster it goes. To turn left, it slows down the beating of its left wing. Sometimes it uses its hind legs as a rudder.

The housefly has sticky pads on its feet which help it to walk upside down on ceilings. It has huge eyes because it flies so quickly it needs to see well to keep from bumping into things. Flies may seem to be very clean because they so often dust their wings and brush their legs, but really they are just about the dirtiest bugs alive.

Houseflies live in, and lay their eggs on garbage and dirt and things that are full of germs which cling to their sticky feet. Then they come into our houses and wipe their dirty feet all over our food, leaving germs behind. That is the way flies spread sickness.

Mosquitoes belong to the fly family. In the summertime they whine about our heads, bite us, and keep us awake at night. Their humming, like the humming of all flies, is the sound of their beating wings. The male mosquito lives on fruit juices. It is the female that bites us and sucks our blood.

Inside her long sucking tube, she has sliding needles sharp enough to bore through our skin. To make our blood thinner and easier to suck, she mixes some of her saliva with it. In the saliva there is a poison which makes bites itch and swell into bumps.

a mosquito that spreads disease

The mosquito lays her eggs on stagnant water. They are all glued to-gether and float like a raft. These eggs, like all other flies' eggs, hatch into larvae called wrigglers. The wrigglers grow into pupae and finally the pupae become grown-up mosquitoes.

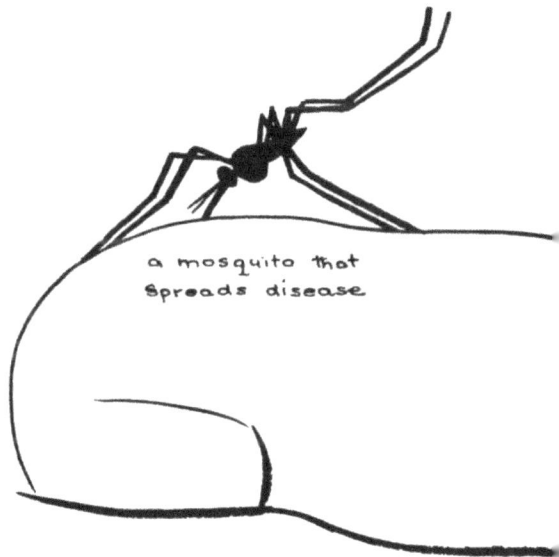

gnat

bot fly

flea

deer fly

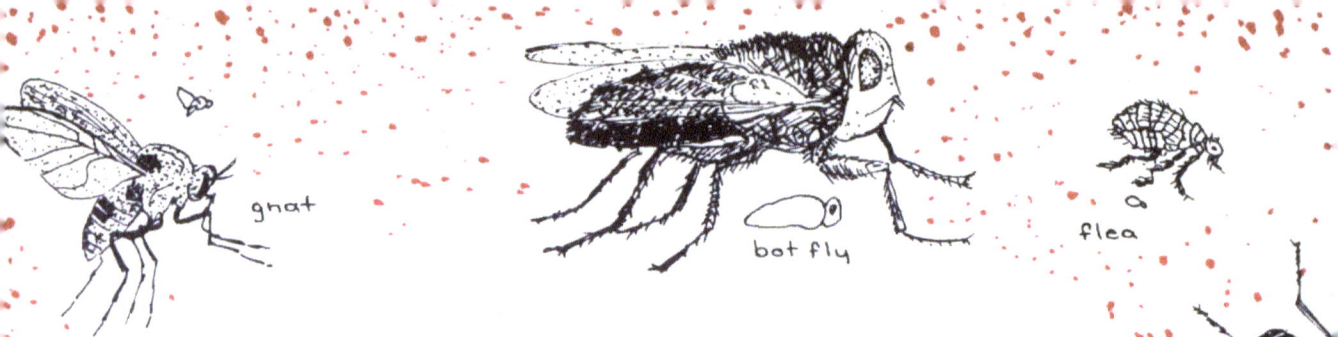

In countries where the climate is very hot, there are mosquitoes that carry about the germs of dreadful diseases. First, the mosquitoes suck up the germs that are in the sick person's blood. Then when they bite someone else for a meal, they leave those germs behind. To get rid of mosquitoes people pour oil on the ponds where they lay their eggs. The hatching mosquitoes can't breathe air through the oil, and they die.

Besides flies that bother us and spread disease, there are flies, called botflies, whose young live in a horse's stomach or under a cow's skin and hurt them.

mosquito

eggs

larva

pupa

A bee fly's children live as unwelcome guests in bees' hives, and eat up the young bees.

The horsefly chases horses and cows. It bites them and makes them switch their tails and stamp their feet.

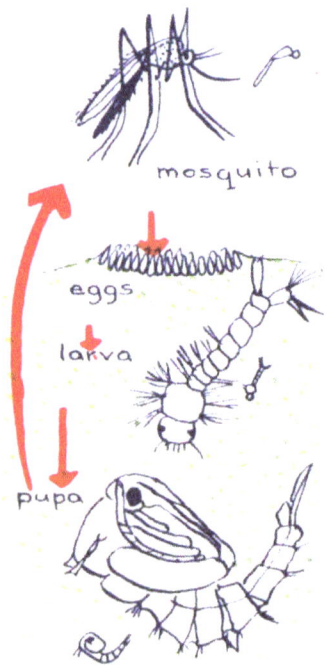

22

(drawings of flies after Suzan N. Swain)

robber fly

bee fly

bluebottle

midge

A deer fly can give people rabbit fever.

A gnat, often called a black fly, bites campers and fishermen in early summer.

A bright blue fly, called a bluebottle, zooms and buzzes about in the summer, too.

The robber fly is the biggest and fiercest of all. It is not afraid of wasps or bees, and swoops down to catch them in mid-air.

A flea is a fly's cousin. Fleas live in dogs' or cats' hair and suck their blood.

A midge, or sand fly, bites you at the beach.

Flies are just about the most bothersome bugs in the world.

about Spiders

The most interesting thing about spiders is that they all spin silk and use it in different ways. Some spiders weave silk rope into webs. Others make silk hinges for the trap doors of their houses. Some spider mothers make soft silk blankets for their young, and most young spiders spin silk balloons with which to go riding on the breeze.

Near the end of a spider's body there are four or more spinning fingers, called spinnerets. Each spinneret has hundreds of tiny holes. Spiders make a liquid inside their bodies, which flows out through the holes and hardens into silk thread in the air. When a spider wants a wide ribbon of silk it spreads its spinnerets far apart and when it wants a thin thread it pulls them close together. A spider sometimes uses the combs which are on its back legs to help it pull wide threads together to make solid sheets of silk.

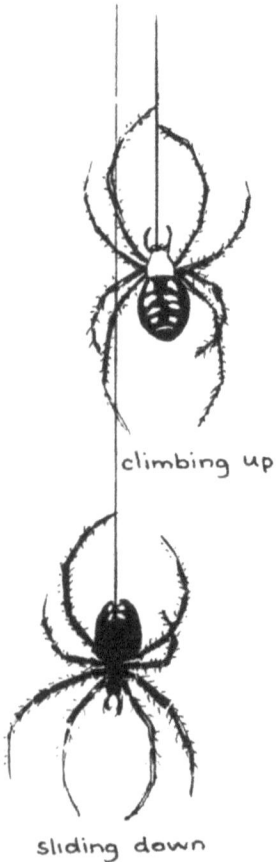

Female spiders are much bigger

climbing up

sliding down

than male spiders. They build the webs, catch the food, and look after the young spiders. But all spiders are very helpful to people, because they feed on bugs that eat up vegetables or trees.

Spiders weave their webs of their sticky silk to catch the juicy grasshoppers and flies and moths they like to eat. A garden spider weaves her web close to the ground where other bugs fly. She weaves it in exactly the same way other garden spiders do, and her first web is just as well made as her tenth. When the web is finished, some spiders make a zig-zag line that looks as if they were signing their names. Though some spiders can repair broken webs, most of them have to start new ones all over again, because they can't pick up an unfinished job part- way through.

Spiders do not get caught in their own webs, because their legs are covered with slippery oil which they make inside their bodies. When a bug gets caught in the snare, the spider shakes thc web with all her might to tangle him even more. She rushes to him and throws blankets of her silk over him, till he can't even wiggle. Then she bites him with her poison fangs and sucks

black widow spider

out his blood.

Spider poison is strong enough to kill small animals, but only some kinds of spider have poison strong enough to hurt people badly. One of these is the Black Widow spider, and you can recognize her by the red hour-glass shape on the underside of her body.

A trap-door spider digs a burrow in the ground and makes a silk-and-mud door to cover it. This door opens and shuts on a silk hinge. She covers the top of the door with earth and leaves and moss, so that from the outside it can hardly be seen. Then she locks the door on the inside by holding it with her sharp claws. This makes her house safe from enemies. Not even water can find a way in. When a juicy bug walks outside, she swings the door back on its hinge, springs out and pounces on him. When she goes for a long walk she trails a

trapdoor spider
in its burrow

26

trapdoor open and shut

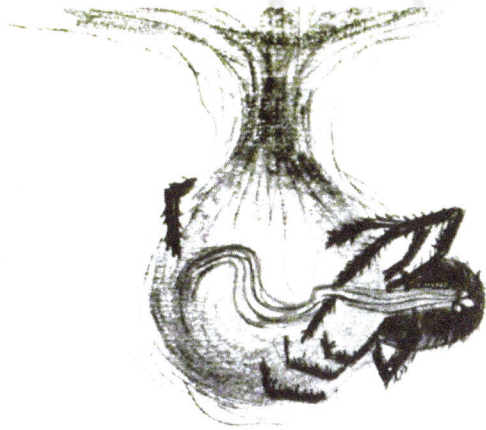
spider building an egg sac
(after H.C. McCook)

line of silk from her burrow, which she follows to find her way back home again.

Most spiders weave satin blankets and soft fluffy quilts for their young. The garden spider weaves a fine satin sac, lays hundreds of eggs in it and wraps the bundle up in clouds of soft silk which she puffs up with the combs on her back legs. Then she hangs her sac to twigs with silk ropes, and the eggs are kept warm in it all winter long.

The tarantula spider also makes a silk sac for her eggs but she carries hers along wherever she goes. Each day she sits in the sun and turns the egg sac round and round to be warmed. When the eggs hatch after a few weeks, the young spiders crawl out onto her back. If they fall off, they use her legs as ladders to climb back.

In the fall, young

spider carrying her egg sac

spiders climb up the tallest grass and shoot out long filmy threads of silk. Some of the threads catch on flowers or bushes and become bridges. The young spiders walk tightrope across the bridges to still higher places, where they send out more threads. The wind tugs at the threads until the spiderlings are lifted high into the air.

They fly over towns and fields, and even across the sea to islands hundreds of miles away. Wherever they land, that's where they grow up.

Balloon-makers, rope-makers, hinge-makers and weavers--spiders, all of them, and all of them spinning their silk.

(after H.C. McCook)

about 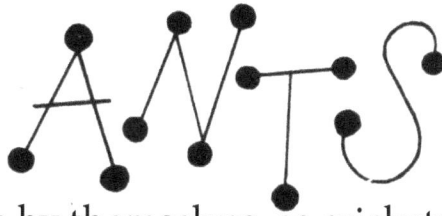 ANTS

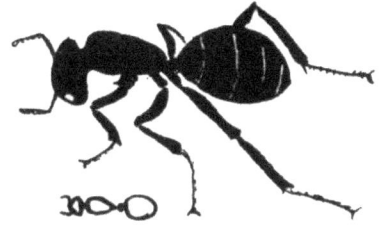
worker

Ants do not live by themselves, as crickets and beetles and most other bugs do. Hundreds and hundreds of them live together in big ant cities and divide up the work to be done. Most of their cities are made of passageways all joined together and winding far under the earth.

larvae

There are three kinds of ants in every ant city--the egg-laying females, the males, and a special group called the workers. The workers are females, but they do not lay eggs. They do all the other work in the city. Each kind of ant is born knowing what his life work is, just as it is born with six legs and a pair of feelers. Ants don't have to be taught how to do their work, any more than a young spider has to be taught how to build a web.

winged female

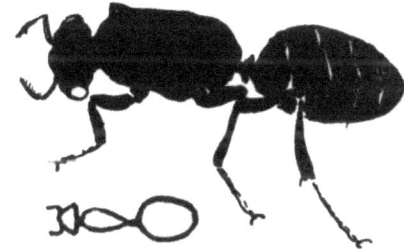
mother

Workers don't have wings, but the males and females do, and they fly together when they mate. This is called swarming. What most people think are a separate breed of "flying ants"

pupa in cocoon

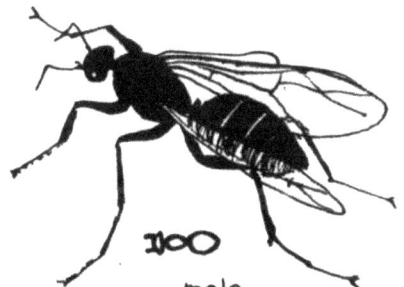
male

are really only the males and females at mating time.

When swarming is over, the male drops to the ground and dies, for his work is done. The female ant then begins her work. She rubs her wings off because she will never need them again.

Then she makes a nest in the earth and lays some eggs. This is the beginning of a new city.

When the eggs hatch, she washes the larvae with her tongue and feeds them the food stored in her stomach and guards them from harm. These first young ants are always tiny workers, who grow up in a few weeks and begin keeping house so that the mother ant need do nothing but lay millons of eggs all the rest of her life. Later, she lays eggs which will grow into males and females as well as workers. It is a mystery even to scientists why her eggs grow into different kinds of ants at different times.

Ants grow up like beetles. They are first eggs, then larvae, then pupae. But young ants can't look after themselves like young beetles. Some of the workers are nursemaids for the young ants. They have to feed them, take them out in the sun for airings, keep them clean and help them change their skins when they grow too big and burst them.

Other workers spend all their lives cleaning the city and adding new parts to it. Some of the workers are bigger than the others. They act like soldiers and policemen, and guard the passages day and night. If danger comes, they run through the city, warning the other ants by tapping their feelers. When they fight, they shoot streams of stinging liquid at their enemies and bite them with their sharp jaws.

Some of the worker ants go out to collect food. Ants like many kinds of food, but their favorite meal is a liquid called honeydew, which they get by milking plant lice. The plant lice make this liquid inside themselves when they suck the juices from trees, just as cows make milk from eating grass. An ant finds a honeydew "cow" and strokes her gently with its feelers. The sweet honeydew comes out of two little tubes at the tip of her

ant milking a honeydew "cow"

body, and the ant sucks it out. It milks one cow after another, till it can't drink another drop. Then it goes back to the city to deliver the honeydew milk to all the other ants. A hungry ant taps the feelers of an ant with food. They touch tongues and honeydew flows from the full ant to the hungry ant.

hungry ant feeding

Besides working hard, ants keep themselves very clean. Ants' bodies are covered with hair so fine it is hard to see. They use their tongues as sponges and their legs with bristles and hooks as combs. Often, before they go to sleep, or after eating, they brush and comb and wash themselves and each other until there isn't a speck of dirt left on them.

Though ants may act like nursemaids or policemen or milkmen they aren't really a bit like people, because they can't think about what they do, or plan their work.

Sometimes that's hard to believe, when you hear the stories that are told about ants.

For example--once upon a time, in Italy, some red ants found their way into a house over a window sill. The lady of the house didn't want them getting into her sugar, so she put some flypaper on the sill to stop them. Soon hundreds of ants were caught.

The next morning, the lady couldn't believe her eyes when she saw a line of ants crossing over the paper and coming into the house again. She looked closer, and discovered that during the night the ants had built a road by dropping bits of earth on the paper. They had not let her stop them!

Scientists have not yet been able to explain just exactly how ants can do such amazing things. There is still so much to learn about a bug's world.

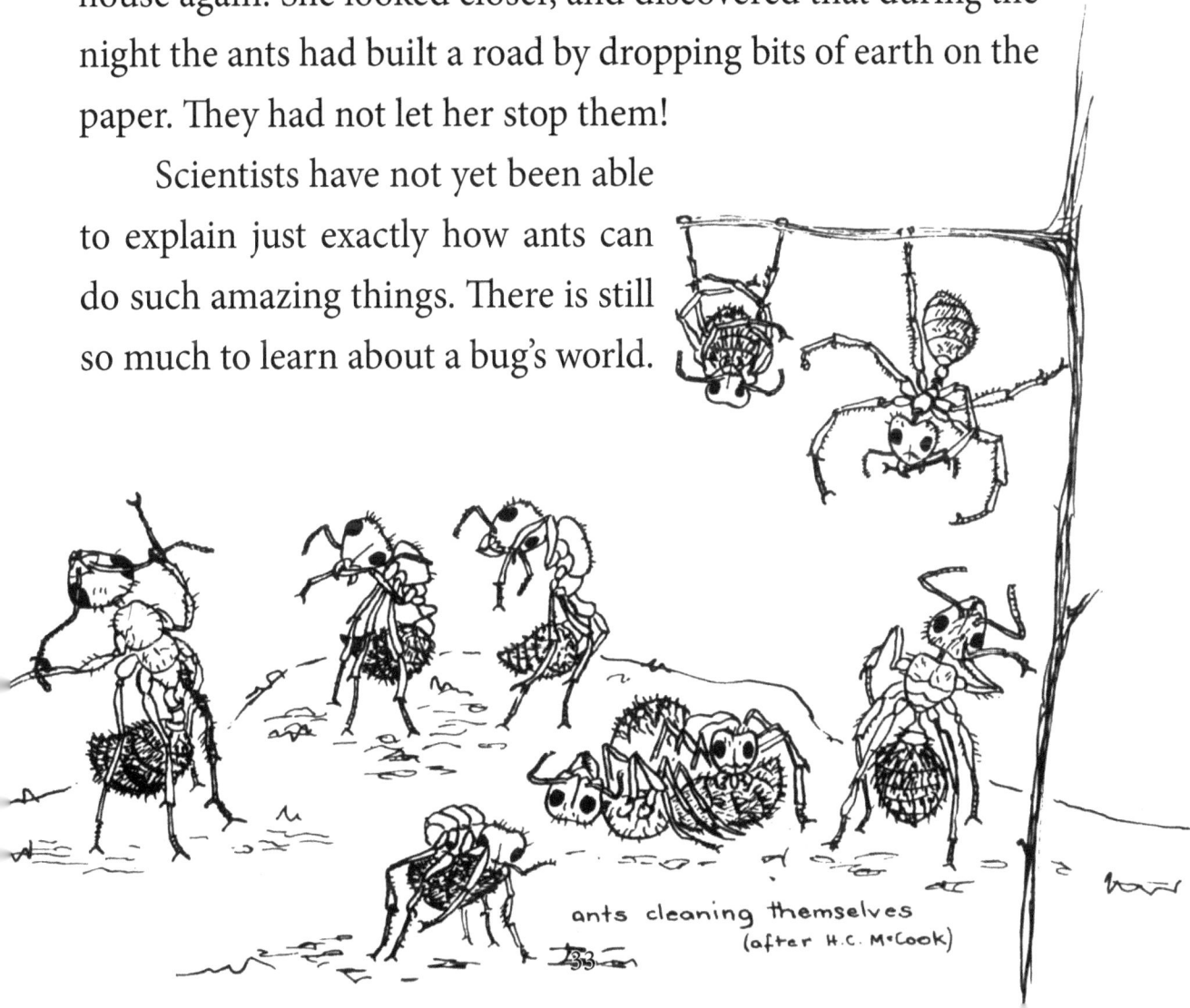

ants cleaning themselves
(after H.C. M'Cook)

Moths and Butterflies

All moths and butterflies have four velvety flying wings. Though they fly slowly, and zig-zag back and forth, they can fly for long distances without getting tired. Some butterflies often fly hundreds of miles south, to escape the winter.

Here's how you can tell moths and butterflies apart. Moths fly at night and usually have feelers that are feathery. Butterflies

eggs

fly in the daytime and have feelers that have knobs on them.

Each family of moths and each family of butterflies is dressed in its own colors and patterns, and lays hundreds of eggs of its own special shape on its own special kind of leaf or twig. The eggs hatch in about a week and a different kind of caterpillar comes out of each kind of egg.

Some caterpillars are as wooly as bears. Some have horns. Some have bristles which sting. Some can wave their heads in the air. One caterpillar has a false-face. It can blow up the front of its body to look like a green snake with yellow eyes.

All caterpillars can spin a silk thread with the spinneret beneath their mouths. Tent caterpillars and pine caterpillars both live in groups, in silk tents they weave for themselves. When pine caterpillars go exploring, they play follow the leader. Each one leaves a silk thread behind, making a ribbon which they all follow home again.

Henri Fabre, a French scientist who has written wonderful stories about his insect friends, once tried an experiment with some pine caterpillars. He joined their silk ribbon end to end in a circle, and they marched around it for eight days, hardly ever stopping. On the eighth day, one caterpillar fell out of line by accident, and found its way home. Then slowly the others followed.

Bugs are born knowing how to do many clever things, but when tricks are played on them they don't know how to figure things out for themselves as people do.

A caterpillar spends all its days just eating. Like the beetle larva, it may grow out of five bigger and bigger skins. The last time it changes its skin, it puts on its new and different pupa skin and goes to sleep.

Most kinds of moth caterpillars

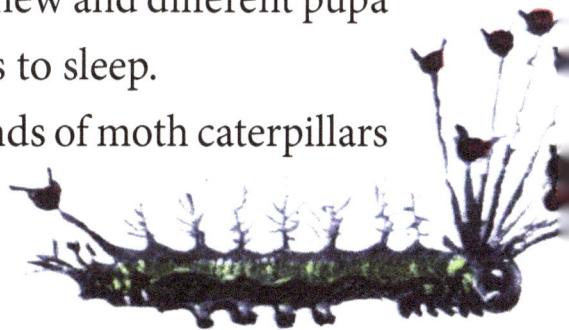

change into their pupa skins in a warm little dressing room they make, called a cocoon. Cocoons may be of silk thread, or of leaves sewn together with silk thread or of earth. People unwind the thread from the cocoon of the silk moth to make silk dresses.

When a butterfly caterpillar becomes a pupa, it doesn't make a cocoon. Instead, it spins a silk net on a twig to give it something to hold on to, and a silk rope to tie itself about the middle. Then it wiggles out of its old caterpillar skin, which has split down the back. The pupa skin underneath is wet and sticky, but when it dries, it is hard and as waterproof as a raincoat. Each kind of butterfly has its own kind of pupa skin.

When the pupa skin splits, the moth or butterfly climbs out. First it dries its wet and wrinkled wings, and then pumps them full of the greenish fluid which is a bug's blood. Then it drinks some flower nectar with its long sucking tongue which works like a nosedropper and can be curled up when it is not being used. After coming out of its pupa skin, it lives only a few more weeks.

a butterfly caterpillar
changes into its pupa skin

During that short time, moths and butterflies do not grow any more. They spend their time fluttering from flower to flower, sipping the sweet juices and having a carefree life.

After the females have mated, they lay their eggs wherever the caterpillars that will hatch from the eggs can find the food they like best to eat.

Grown-up moths and butterflies are quite harmless. It is while they are in their caterpillar stages that they do damage. The moth caterpillars are the worst pests. They are the ones that tunnel through fruit, and stalks of grain, and eat holes in our best woolen sweaters.

Moths and butterflies have many enemies. Birds think them a juicy mouthful and find their colors easy to follow in a chase. But they each have a way to fool their enemies at such times. A butterfly's brightest colors are on the top of its wings. When a butterfly alights, it folds its wings above its back and, presto, the bright colors are hidden. Only the dull undersides of the wings show, and they match the surroundings. When a moth rests, it folds its front wings over the more brightly colored rear ones. In that way, it too becomes part of the background, and can escape the sharpest eyes.

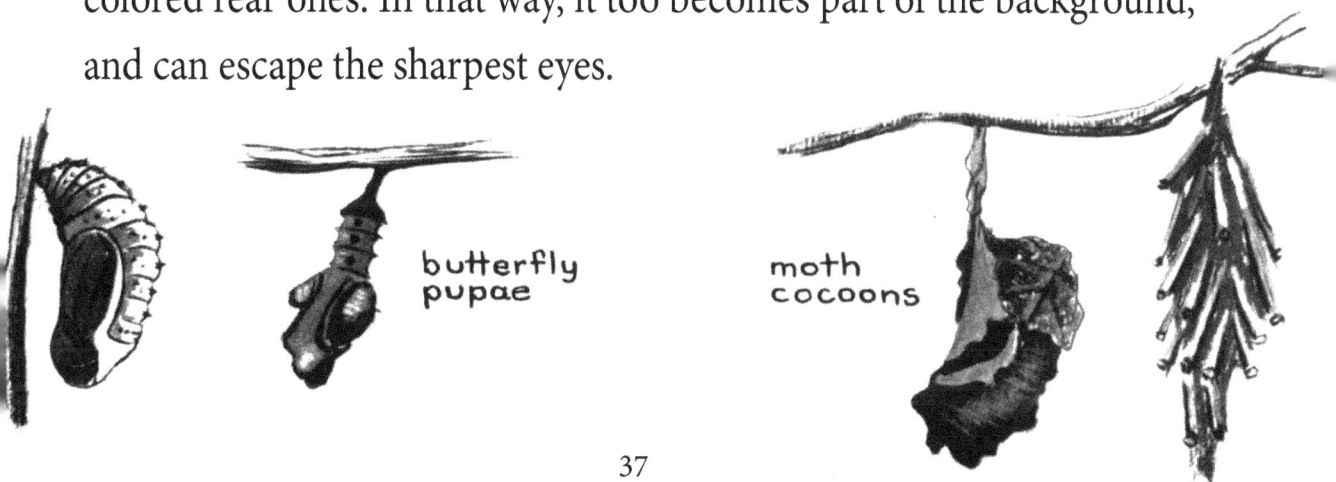

butterfly
pupae

moth
cocoons

red admiral butterfly

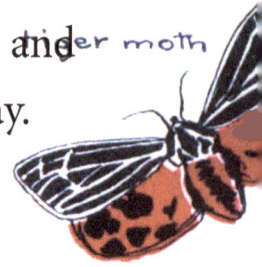

tiger moth

Here are some of the moths and butterflies you may meet some day.

io moth

acraea moth

large orange sulphur

wandering comma butterfly

white butterfly resting

luna moth resting

viceroy butterfly

WASPS and BEES

Wasps and bees build houses to protect their young. Some wasp and bee mothers work all alone to build separate nurseries for each of their eggs.

A mud-dauber wasp builds small round rooms of the mud she collects from puddles, and lays an egg in each one. She fills each room full of spiders which she has stung to sleep with her stinger. The spiders are still alive but they can't feel or move. That is how a wasp keeps its food fresh until it is ready to be eaten.

When the egg hatches into a grub, it eats the sleeping spiders until it is grown up and able to catch food for itself.

The mother carpenter bee makes a tunnel in wood. The separate nurseries for each egg are separated by walls which she makes of sawdust mixed with her saliva. She leaves a tiny loaf of bee-bread, made of honey and pollen, for each grub to eat until it grows up and bores its way through to the outside world.

There are other wasps, and also bees, who live and work together and build large houses with many nurseries for their young.

carpenter bee

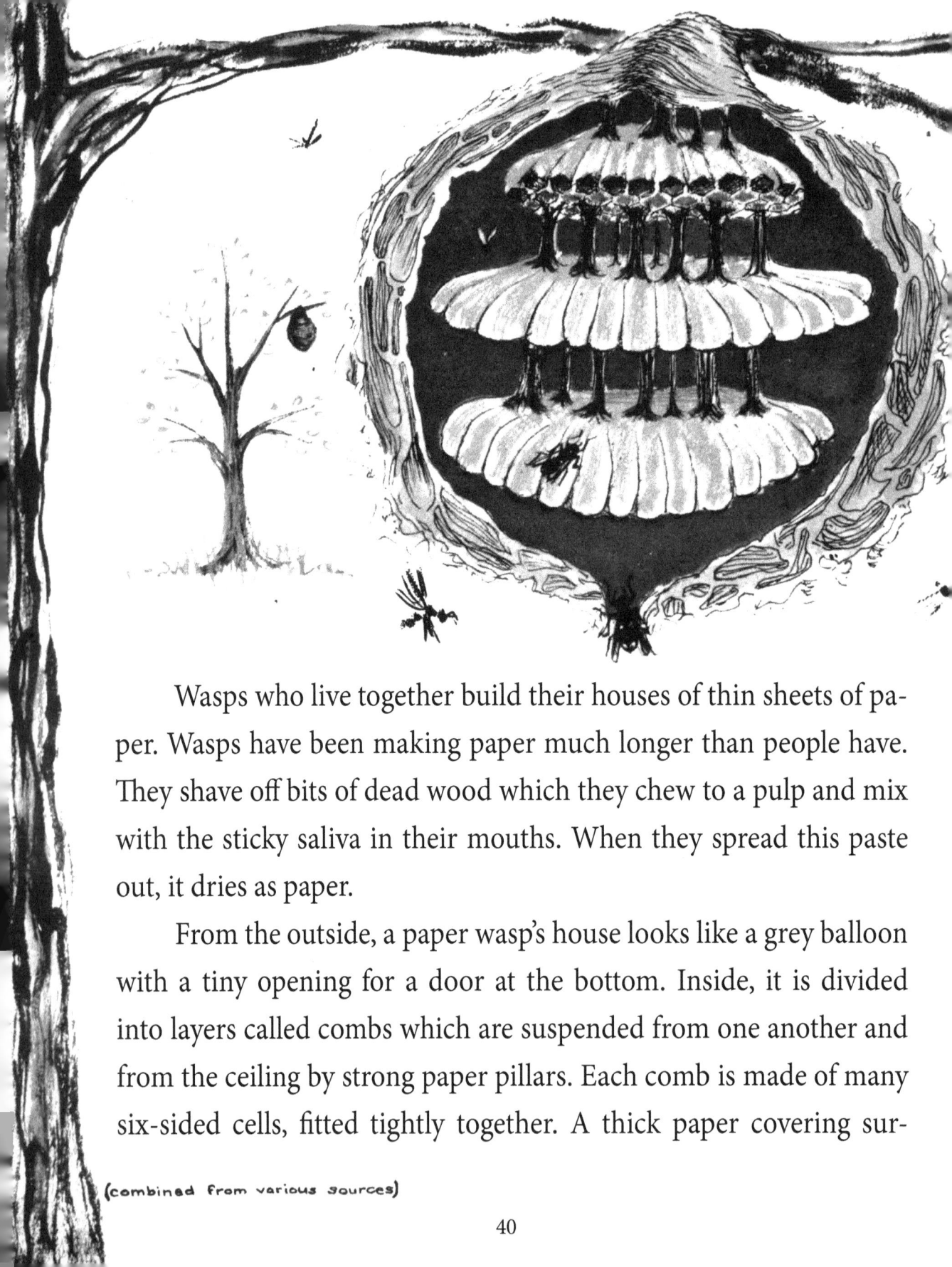

Wasps who live together build their houses of thin sheets of paper. Wasps have been making paper much longer than people have. They shave off bits of dead wood which they chew to a pulp and mix with the sticky saliva in their mouths. When they spread this paste out, it dries as paper.

From the outside, a paper wasp's house looks like a grey balloon with a tiny opening for a door at the bottom. Inside, it is divided into layers called combs which are suspended from one another and from the ceiling by strong paper pillars. Each comb is made of many six-sided cells, fitted tightly together. A thick paper covering sur-

(combined from various sources)

rounds all the combs. It protects the nest and keeps out rain and cold.

A young mother wasp starts to build the nest and makes a comb, where she lays her eggs. The eggs hatch into grubs which she feeds every day. They have big sucking feet to hold them in their up-side-down cells, for if they fall out, they have no way to get back, and they die.

But the grubs that are able to hold on, eat and grow big. They make paper caps for their cells and go to sleep as pupae inside. Later they creep out as worker wasps who take over the housekeeping duties from their mother. As the family grows, they build more combs inside the nest. Then, bit by bit, they enlarge the paper covering of their nest by scraping paper off the inside and plastering it on the outside, and by adding new material. They catch insects and make them into a paste to feed the newly hatched grubs.

Near the end of the summer, the mother wasp lays eggs which grow into males, called drones, and females. The males and females mate. Then, when the cold weather comes, all the wasps in the nest die except the young females. They sleep in some cozy spot during the winter, and each one may begin a new wasp's nest in the spring.

Wasps live in their nests only in the summertime, and they do not use an old nest over again an-other year.

eggs  larvae  pupae in capped cells

eggs

grubs

queen cell

drone (male)

quee[n]

wor[ker]

empt[y] cell

Wild honeybees live together and build their combs inside old tree trunks. People who raise bees build small houses, called hives in which the bees make their own combs.

All bees' combs are divided into six-sided cells like those of wasps, but they are made of wax. Many bees share in building them even from the very beginning. Worker bees make wax inside themselves out of the flowering nectar and pollen they eat, though no one knows how. They squeeze the wax through slots in their stomachs and chew the wax and mix it with saliva. Then each worker takes a turn at shaping the wax into cells.

There is only one queen bee in each hive and she lays all the eggs, one in each cell. When the eggs hatch, the worker nursemaids feed the grubs bee-bread and keep them clean.

While the nursemaids are busy with the young bees, oth-

er workers fly busily back and forth from the fields of clover and the flower gardens. They collect nectar with their long tongues and make it into honey inside them-selves and collect pollen in the "market baskets" on their hind legs. Still other workers pack the honey and pollen into storage cells for the bees to eat in the wintertime.

modern beehive

The male bees, called drones, do not collect food and have no stings to defend themselves. In the fall, when the mating season is over and the honey stores must be saved for the winter, the drones are driven from the hive to die.

When the beehive gets too crowded, big, pear-shaped cells are built where the special queen eggs are laid. The queen grubs which hatch from the eggs are fed a special royal jelly to make them grow larger than all the others. Then, before the first grown-up new queen has crept from her cell, the old queen, who may live for several years, flies away with workers to start a new hive somewhere else. The first young queen to be born be- comes the new mother of the old hive.

worker with full "market basket"

more BUGS

There are many other exciting bugs. There's the daddy-long-legs, which has eight of the longest legs of any bug. There is the millipede, which has dozens of legs yet runs slowly and curls up into a ball when it is frightened.

Perhaps one day you reached for a twig -- and it walked away from you. That was a bug called a walking stick.

Maybe you've been frightened by the fierce praying mantis, which is the only bug that can turn its head about as you can. It doesn't hurt people, but it snatches hornets or beetles or bees out of the air with its spiny front legs. In Japan, the praying mantis is often tied to a bedpost, to catch mosquitoes at night.

The water strider can skate. Its legs skim over the water and its shadow chases behind it on the bottom of the pool.

Then there are the tiny tree hoppers, which have faces like Hallowe'en masks, as you can see if you look at them under a magnifying glass.

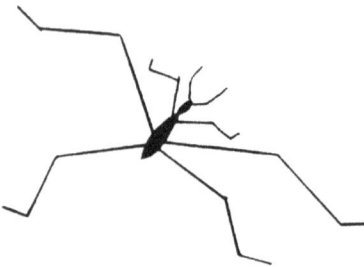

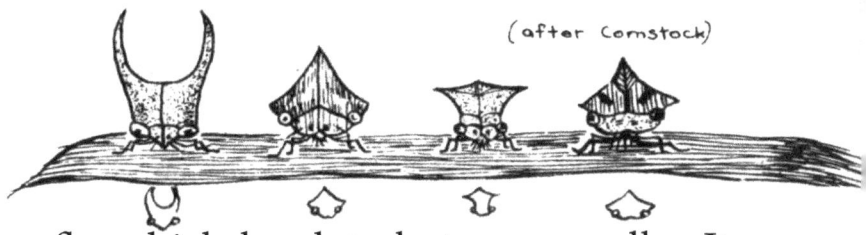

There is the dragonfly, which has legs but never walks. It swoops through the air at sixty miles an hour. It may hurt if it bumps into you, but it never stings or bites people.

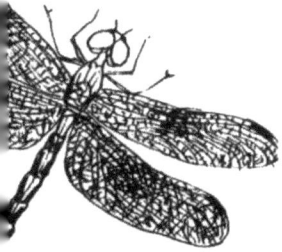

An ant lion digs itself a pit in the sand and buries itself at the bottom with only its jaws sticking out. When bugs slip down the steep sloping sides, they are caught in its waiting jaws!

The caddis fly's larva lives and breathes under water like a fish. It builds itself a case for protection, out of bits of sand and shells and pebbles cemented together with the silk it spins.

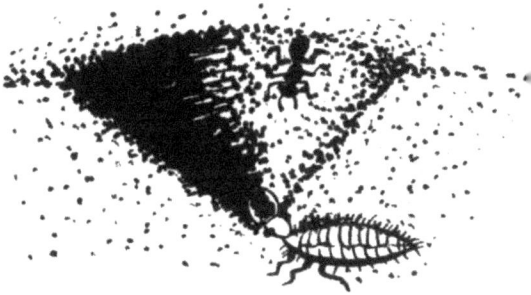

Some day you will meet the bugs in this book again, and you will be meeting lots and lots of new bugs, too. Perhaps you can discover their secrets if you open your eyes and ears and wait and watch.

Bugs Bugs

Everywhere

www.ingramcontent.com/pod-product-compliance
Lightning Source LLC
Chambersburg PA
CBHW042336030426

42335CB00028B/3364